Love

A Hidden Treasure
(in plain sight)

Copyright © 2014 Calvin L. Emerson
All rights reserved

ISBN: 978-0-9833516-4-1

Published by Willoughby Press
Owosso, Michigan 48867

Permissions

Scriptures taken from the Holy Bible, New International Version® , NIV.® Copyright© 1973, 1978, 1984, 2011 by Biblica, Inc.™ Used by permission of Zondervan. All rights reserved worldwide. www.zondervan.com The "NIV" and "New International Version" are trademarks registered in the United States Patent and Trademark Office by Biblica, Inc. ™

"Yet Lord, I also thank you. . . " from THIRTY ONE DAYS OF PRAISE: ENJOYING GOD ANEW by Ruth Myers, copyright © 1994, 1996, 1997, 2003 by Ruth Myers and Warren Myers. Used by permission of WaterBrook Multnomah, an imprint of the Crown Publishing Group, a Division of Random House LLC. All rights reserved.

Permission granted to use "nine styles of worship" from SACRED PATHWAYS by Gary Thomas (Zondervan)

Permission granted by Pam Pugh, Managing Editor for Moody Publishers, to use excerpts from Man: The Dwelling Place of God By A. W. Tozer.

Acknowledgments

I would like to thank my brother in law, **Ross Woodstock**, who has been most encouraging with my first book and again in this "Love" book. I highly respect his writing talents and opinion on my progression of thoughts.

James McKay has been Vice Chairman of my board for 28 years. He has read through both writings and has offered valuable insight. As a man of God I respect his thoughts.

Celia Woodworth looks at editing from a journalists point of view. Her insights assure that the book will be readable. She has been invaluable to me.

Colleen Sheedlo is a perfectionist in editing. She has saved me from much embarrassment and I appreciate her.

Rev. Glen Pettigrove has been a close friend for over thirty four years. He is a master at using examples and illustrations as he preaches. He has taught me how to make my thoughts clear by using illustrations.

My wife **Beverly** has typed the entire book. She has suffered much eye fatigue trying to interpret my hand writing. I thank God she has patience and the ability to understand the "Calvin Language".

Dedication

I am dedicating **LOVE, A Hidden Treasure (in plain sight)** to my beautiful wife, Beverly. Even though I share stories in the book of how gifted we are at trashing love, Beverly has stood beside me during all of the hard circumstances we have had to face. Her love and encouragement has given me confidence to do things I thought impossible.

I do not pretend to be a polished author, yet she encouraged me to write. I sensed God calling me from a high paying career into the ministry and to a church with only fifteen people attending. She supported me 100%. When I shared my dream to build a new home with our sons, she swallowed hard but then came along side and worked as hard as we did.

Love between two human beings is so imperfect, but I have sensed a special connection to my wife.

"Her children rise up and call her blessed; her busband also and he praised her: Many women do noble things, but you surpass them all."

Proverbs 31:28-29

Table of Content

Acknowledgements *3*

Dedication *4*

Introduction: Love, Hurt, Hate Cycle *7*

Chapter

1	*Trashing The Treasure* *15*
2	*The Perfect Treasure* *27*
3	*What Does The Treasure Look Like?* ... *39*
4	*The Treasure Map Part 1* *55*
5	*The Treasure Map Part 2* *73*
6	*The Treasure Map Part 3* *81*
7	*The Treasure Beyond The Narrow Gate* . *89*
8	*Guarding The Treasure* *101*
9	*Sharing The Treasure* *111*
10	*Epilogue* *119*

LOVE, A HIDDEN TREASURE

Introduction

If I were to ask you what one of your greatest emotional needs is in this life, I'm confident you would respond, "the need to be loved". We all desire to be loved. Love is what makes life worth living. We desire people to love us even if we do not feel beautiful and far from perfect. We desire people to love us when we do not feel lovable. Love is something we cannot live without. It is what drives our engines, and it helps us get through the hard times.

I have personally discovered that love is more precious than success, wealth, worldly posessions, and even more precious than popularity. Love is of greater value than gold and silver. Love is a treasure. It is a treasure of great worth. It is a treasure in plain sight, yet it is hidden from most of the world.

My first venture with love came in the summer between 7th and 8th grade. I met this beautiful girl in school, and she just melted my heart. I remember getting my year book and rushing out to the car to show her picture to my mom. Mom said she had beautiful "horned rimmed" glasses, because the rest of her picture was a little faint.

During that summer she invited me to go on a hayride. Full of excitement I accepted, anticipating the most beautiful evening of my life. That invitation was proof she had the same feelings for me that I had for her. I just knew she was about to become my lifelong partner.

As I arrived at her farm I realized I knew very few people; but that did not matter. I was in love. But then the evening quickly fell apart. As we prepared to get on the wagon there was another boy, a year older than

INTRODUCTION

me, who helped my love onto the wagon. My heart broke. Obviously 8th graders knew a whole lot more about romance than 7th graders. I'll have to admit that in the seventh grade my idea of love was perhaps only half a step above pulling pigtails. It was the longest hayride I have ever been on. I tried to be upbeat --- throwing straw at mailboxes as we passed them by --- watching my love hold hands with another boy. After the hayride Mom picked me up and asked if I had a good time. I told her, "Yes", not wanting her to know I had been stood up by the beautiful girl in the horned rimmed glasses.

That same spring our house burned, and dad thought it would be an adventure for all eight of us to camp out in the back yard for the whole summer. Our bedroom was a 16' x 16' army tent with seven beds crowded together. The next morning my mom, once again, asked me what had happened at the hayride? Again, I told her that I had a good time. Her response was, "Oh, I was just wondering because you cried all night long." My heart was broken, but I had no idea I cried in my sleep. I guess it's pretty hard to hide your emotions when eight people are sleeping in one crowded tent.

That was my first experience with a broken heart. Up until that time I was the one to break the hearts, now mine was broken. Love can deal us some harsh blows over the years. It can start out very exciting with our heart racing and then, for no reason at all, just simply turn sour. We all want to be loved, but we all have had disappointing experiences with love. We may even feel there is no one out there to love us the way we desire to be loved. Love always seems to be both wonderful and disappointing.

To complete my story about the beautiful girl in the horn rimmed glasses, I have to fast forward eleven years. This girl finally regained her sanity. She decided she

INTRODUCTION

had made the mistake of her life on the hay ride, and eleven years later she ***married me***. I'm not sure what happened the night of the hayride. Obviously she wasn't in her right mind. But whatever the seventh grade problem was, we are now celebrating 46 years of marriage. They have been wonderful years, and yet disappointing years at the same time.

Love seems to be so imperfect. How can one human being love another at one moment and then break their heart the next? How can I love my wife one moment and then be angry enough to walk away from the marriage the next? My wife is beautiful and kind hearted. Yet why does she upset me so much at times, and why do I upset her? She always said she wanted to marry her knight in shining armor. After we were married a few years she told me my armor was starting to tarnishing.

Some people just put up with the "love,

anger, hate cycle" and experience a lower form of love than God ever created us to experience. We become satisfied with a mediocre kind of love. Yet God wants us to experience a beautiful, almost perfect love. Love is a hidden treasure. Thus very few will ever find it. Back in the 60's the Everly Brothers wrote a hit song that shares this feeling well. It is titled "When Will I Be Loved?" Following are two of the verses:

> *"I've been cheated,*
> *Been mistreated.*
> *When will I be Loved?*
> *I've been made blue,*
> *I've been lied to.*
> *When will I be loved?"*

Everyone wants to be loved and yet, love is so elusive. It's so sad. The road to love is very clearly laid out and sought after by so many. But very few will ever find it.

So how do we discover this perfect love our hearts just ache to experience? Where

INTRODUCTION

can we learn about its qualities? Is there even such a thing as perfect love? Yes there is, and I have found a book that will define what perfect love looks like, where to find it, and how to keep it. It will even teach us how to love "unlovable people". As you read, you will discover how easy it is to love and be loved. But be prepared to change your understanding of what love truly looks like. Love is a hidden treasure, and yet it is in plain sight.

But before we look into the perfect love we all desire, let us explore a lower form of love with which we all seem to be satisfied.

LOVE, A HIDDEN TREASURE

Chapter 1
Trashing The Treasure

It is true. We usually settle for a much lower form of love than God intended for us to experience on this earth. In the Greek language, this lower form of love is called Philia love. It is a "give and take" form of love and is the only love most people will ever experience on this earth. It is defined as follows: I will love you as long as you are pleasing to me. If you are not pleasing, I will withdraw my love.

It is so easy to love someone who is kind hearted and loving towards us. But, just once, let them turn their back on us; and we tend to withdraw our love from them, even if only for a moment. Most people put up with this kind

LOVE, A HIDDEN TREASURE

of love, because it is the only love they have ever known.

Friendships are broken because of harsh words spoken or because of misunderstandings. Marriages are ruined when one partner does something that hurts the one they love. Sometimes in a marriage we do things that are really dumb, and a partner is hurt so deeply they cannot overcome the scars.

The fact is real. The more intimate we become in a relationship, the more ability we have to hurt that person. The more we try to love, the greater is our ability to trash that love. Sigmund Freud described this dilemma as the "porcupine theory". He states, "Despite goodwill, human intimacy cannot occur without substantial mutual harm, resulting in cautious behavior and weak relations." He further states, "This dilemma is used to explain introversion and isolationism." The more I am hurt by people the more I will shy away from people.

A porcupine will try to get close to another porcupine just to receive more body heat on a cold day. However, the closer they get, the greater the possibility that the quills of one will hurt the hide of another. The porcupine will then separate and try again later. We, as humans, are social beings. God created us to need each other and to have relationships with each other. Yet, by being social, we expose ourselves to being hurt.

I stuck a quill deep into her heart.

I love my wife dearly but in the early part of our marriage I had no idea what her emotional needs were. I had become fairly successful in business, and I lived each day to become more successful. My career was in sales. I felt there was not a greater profession in the world than selling and traveling. I was not tied down to a desk with someone looking over my shoulder every day. I loved traveling across Michigan on the back roads just to

LOVE, A HIDDEN TREASURE

experience the rural areas I loved so much.

I enjoyed going to the big cities, competing with some of the best salesmen in my industry. Because it was in the big cities, I made a lot of money. Yet I loved leaving in the afternoon to return to the rural areas. My life was amazing! I was working with some very upbeat people and even some professional athletes. I was making a real comfortable living and traveling to different stores every day.

In the midst of all of the excitement I was experiencing and in the early days of our marriage, my wife asked me the question, "Do you think about me during your busy day?" At the time our marriage was going through some difficult times, and I simply responded, "No".

I stuck a quill deep into her heart, and I regret it to this day. She was very emotional and vulnerable in asking the question, and I recklessly trashed her emotions. In essence she was asking me to comfort her and display my deep love and need for her. She was asking me if she was more important to me than my wonderful career. She wanted to be assured that our love would last through all eternity. She wanted me to answer yes, but instead I just slapped her in the face with a "no". The older I get and the more I try to understand my wife's needs, the more I cringe at my cold hearted response. If I could just live that day over, I could heal a lot of hurt I sent deep into her heart. I trashed the treasure.

She stuck a quill deep into my ego.

We are so good at trashing the treasure. The closer we get to each other, the greater our ability to hurt each other. Another incident happened that we are both able to laugh at now, but at the time it was devastating. We had just recently become Christians and started giving money to a place called Youth Haven Ranch.

LOVE, A HIDDEN TREASURE

Each year the ranch had a banquet to celebrate what God was doing and to thank those who faithfully gave. As we walked into the banquet room one year, we were graciously welcomed by the owners, Morry and Dorothy Carlson. Morry called one of the workers over and told him to escort us up to the head table. My head began to spin, and my ego took off like a NASA rocket. We were seated at the head table set for only four people, Morry, Dorothy, my wife, and me. What a tremendous honor.

As our dinner wound down, I talked to my wife about the honor we had been given that evening. I thought, perhaps it was because of the money we had donated. She looked over at me and said, "You do not sit at the head table unless you are the keynote speaker." At the time, we were experiencing some difficulty in our marriage, and she just "forgot" to tell me that I was to be the keynote speaker that evening. I wonder if three hundred and fifty people at the dinner saw my jaw drop and actually bounce off the table.

I leaned over and asked Morry if he wanted me to say something, and he responded with a funny look on his face, "Well yes, you are the keynote speaker this evening." I began to wonder why everyone in the room knew about this assignment except me. I panicked! Three hundred and fifty people and I am about to make a blundering fool of myself. There was no place to run and no place to hide. I had about fifteen minutes to put a twenty minute speech together. Have you ever noticed how difficult it is to think logical thoughts when your mind is in panic mode?

The speech was short, and I would guess some of the guests were relieved because it was short. On the drive home my wife and I **TALKED**! I won't say there was any yelling in the car --- we just **TALKED**.

She explained later that she knew I enjoyed speaking to audiences, and she just didn't want me to get nervous. Yet that was a sharp quill that bypassed my heart and went deep into my ego. Old Mr. Porcupine had a heyday separating us that evening.

We have a great potential to hurt each other.

The closer we get to each other the greater potential we have for hurting each other. The more we try to love each other the more we end up trashing our love. Then, the more we are hurt and the more we feel unloved, the more we become introverted, not wanting to be around people even though we have this deep inner need to be social.

I would guess that is why many people hold friendships at arms length. They have been hurt too many times in relationships to risk another venture into love. Others may venture into another relationship only to hold back a large quantity of intimacy, and that is yet another way of trashing a relationship.

Is there such a thing as love, real love, deep and intimate love? Is there a treasure called love? Is there something called perfect love? If there is, where do we find it? Yes, there is a perfect love, but it is hidden from most people, even though it is in plain sight. Most people will experience the porcupine theory in relationships. They will love, get hurt, withdraw, try again, get hurt again, and the cycle goes on and on. As each love experience draws to a close because of hurt, we open up our hearts less in the next relationship and thus experience less love.

To illustrate this dilemma about love, I will use the picture of a line. Point B represents me, and point C would be my wife, a friend, a neighbor or anyone I am trying to draw close. In this example, I am going to say point "C" represents my wife because she has been my love and my best friend for a very long period of time.

$$\underset{\text{Me}}{\text{B}\underline{\qquad}} \quad \underset{\text{My Wife}}{\underline{\qquad}\text{C}}$$

As illustrated before, the closer I move toward her and the more I try to love her, the more I am capable of hurting her. I am an imperfect human being, and so I love imperfectly. Then when I hurt her, by telling her I don't think about her during the day, she withdraws a lot of her emotions from me. She doesn't do this to be mean, but she does it just to protect her own self worth. Thus, you will notice on the drawing, the line between us is broken. This broken line represents an imperfect love.

Later, she doesn't tell me I am the keynote speaker at a banquet with 350 people in attendance, then I withdraw some of my emotions from her. Once again the line between us is severed. We have been married forty-six years and we just cannot seem to get beyond those moments where we hurt each other. She does not do it intentionally because she is a very kind-hearted woman, but it just seems to happen.

So here I am, an imperfect human being, trying to love my wife in a beautiful and perfect way, and I fail. Then, there she is, an imperfect person, trying to love me in a perfect way, and she fails. The line between B and C will always be a broken line, because my wife and I are both incapable of perfect love.

We simply cannot share a satisfying love.

Sadly I have come to the conclusion that if my wife cannot love me the way I desire to be loved, there is no one on the face of this earth who is capable of loving me. If there is a perfect love on this earth, it must be a hidden treasure. Maybe it is out there, but it does not seem to be readily available. It is out there, but it is hidden.

My problem is that I want a perfect love, but I am only capable of sharing a self-

LOVE, A HIDDEN TREASURE

gratifying kind of love. I want people to love me no matter what kind of sour mood I might be in. When I am hurt I withdraw my love. What I need to discover is a source of love. I am not a source of love, I am a sponge and am only capable of absorbing love.

Is there such a thing as a deep, intimate love? Is there such a thing as a source of love? Yes there is, and we can all find it. But it is found in places that we seldom venture. Before we answer these questions, let us take a moment and see what that perfect love looks like and decide if it is worth chasing after?

Chapter 2
The Perfect Treasure

I really desire to be loved. I want someone to love me when I am good and when I mess up. I want to be loved when I look sharp and when I look ridiculous. I desire to be loved when I feel tenderhearted and when I feel unlovable. I just cannot seem to find that perfect love as I walk on this earth.

Is perfect love available, or do I just have to put up with people who break my heart without even realizing what they are doing? Maybe I am looking in all the wrong places. In reality I am looking for a "source of love", someone from whom love would continually flow no matter what circumstances surrounded it.

When I was eleven years old, my dad asked me to help him cut some lumber at a portable sawmill. There were six kids in the family, and I suppose this was my way of gaining his attention. Dad was a gifted sawyer, and I always enjoyed watching him work. But, on this assignment it felt like it was 100 degrees below zero, and the wind was howling. I could not, for the life of me, stay warm.

Finally, after a "tiny bit" of complaining, my dad ordered me to go sit in the car and get warm. That was a wonderful idea, except that the heater in that car did not work. In fact, I don't think the heater ever worked in that old Studebaker from the time he bought it.

The inside of the car was as cold, if not colder than the outside. Sitting in the car was like sitting in a freezer trying to get warm. I needed a source of heat to get warm and not a freezer. What I needed was a bonfire that I could approach, take off my gloves and warm my hands and my whole being. A bonfire would be a source of heat. If dad would have just built a bonfire instead of sending me to the car, I might have gotten warm. A bonfire may have burned down the whole sawmill, but I really didn't care. It was an old shed and I needed heat, the more heat the better.

To get warm I needed a source of heat. To find love I need to discover a source of love. Dating someone in high school or college was my idea of love but it was not a source of love because it was the old cycle of love, hurt, dislike, and then try to love again.

A number of years ago, as a Pastor, I was counseling with a couple who were struggling in their marriage. As I talked with one party, it was very apparent they were not feeling loved by the other. Then as I spoke with the other, they felt the same way. Neither felt loved.

Neither of them were a source of love. Each party was capable of absorbing love, but, neither was the source. Each one wanted to be perfectly loved by the other. When they were not, they felt unloved. They were hungry to experience love. I use this couple as an example, not because their problem is rare but, because they are more like the norm in our world today. People are hungry to be loved, but rarely experience real love.

Everyone desires to be loved, but no one seems to be capable of becoming the source of love. Just as I needed to find a source of heat on that cold day with my dad, so we need to discover the source of love to feel loved. So where do we find this source of love? To find it I am going to a book that has never lied to me or led me astray. It has always been encouraging, and it is a book full of truth. It is written with love, by a God who desires only the very best for his children: the same as I desire only the best for my children. This book is the Bible.

In 1 John 4 the author is addressing a church having a difficult time and experiencing division. I'm not sure whether they were arguing over which camel to use as a Sunday School bus or whether to use big megaphones or little megaphones for their sound system. Whatever the problem was, the apostle John approached them in a very gentle manner. Instead of pointing his finger at one side or the other, trying to point out the source of the conflict, John concentrates on the remedy.

That remedy is to love one another, which is so difficult to do in the heat of a conflict. Rather than telling them it is a law to love one another, and they must obey the law, John focuses on how to love one another. John tells the church that in order to love one another they must approach the source of love. In I John 4:7-8 he defines that source of love as follows:

"Dear Friends, let us love one another, for love comes from God. Everyone who loves has been born

of God and knows God. Who ever does not love does not know God, because God is love."

God is love. God is The source of love. There is a source of love in this world. Just as heat comes from a fire, love comes from God. I am not the source of love. My wife is not the source of love. My friends in Kiwanis are not the source of love. In all of literature written I do not know of any that states that someone else is THE source of love. Maybe they are a loving people, but not the source of love. God is the only one who is THE source of love.

To be loved, I must approach the source of love. Relationships fail because each person in the relationship expects the other to be the source of love, and they are not. Yes, I am able to love other people if they pour out their love upon me - - - if I can sense complete love coming from them. When complete love doesn't come from others (and it never will) I am prone to withdraw my love for a time.

Now, let me complete the line drawing in chapter one by including the source of love. I am at point 'B' and the person I am trying to love is at point 'C'.

As you recall, the line between us is broken because when I am hurt, I withdraw my love, or at least withdraw my emotions from the relationship for a period of time. Then, the person at point "C" reacts the exact same way when they are hurt.

But look at the completed drawing with point "A" representing God.

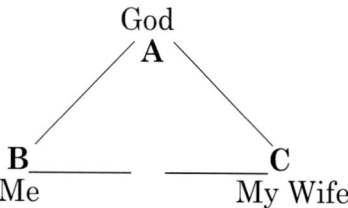

The vector from point A to B comes into place when I have a relationship with God. Notice, it is not a broken line. Vector AB can never be broken because God is the source of love. I may not live up to His expectations (which happens often). I may not always be perfectly obedient. I may even break His heart at times, but, no matter what, it is impossible for Him to withdraw His love from me because He is the source of love.

All love comes from God and continually flows from Him. God is love. His love is there for everyone, whether they are perfectly Holy, or struggling to live up to His expectations. As you experience more heat the closer you get to a bonfire, you will experience more love the closer you get to God. He cannot possibly withdraw His love from you, because, His love is a part of His DNA.

Then that perfect love He has for me continually draws me closer and closer to Him. It is beautiful to my heart. It is something I am hungry to experience. It is such a blessing to me because I have never experienced that quality of love before. On this earth I have to act proper to earn someone's love. I have to do things that are pleasing to them. I have to earn their love. But on vector A-B I will never have to do things to earn it. I don't have to be perfect or always pleasing. It is pure and eternal and will never be withdrawn.

Let me point out one more thing this drawing illustrates. The closer I move towards God and the more of His love I experience, the more love I am able to pour out on my wife. Then, the closer she moves toward God and the more love she experiences, the more love she is able to pour out on me. The adjusted triangle reveals that we are able to love each other more, the closer we move toward God.

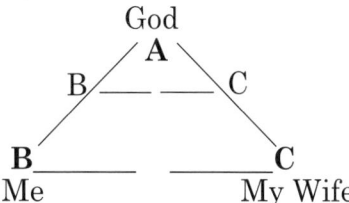

Plus, the more we both experience God's love, the smaller the gap between us becomes. We begin to share a greater love and are less prone to hurt each other.

Does God love everyone on earth?

Some may ask, "If God is the source of love, doesn't He love everyone perfectly?" The answer is yes. God loves every person on the face of this earth. But, if they are not walking hand in hand with God, if they don't have a relationship with Him, if they are not communicating with Him continually, how will they know about His love, let alone experience it. It would be like me trying to get warm by never even approaching the bonfire. It cannot be done. I must approach the bonfire to get warm. I must approach God to experience His love.

Acts 3:19 gives us a picture of what we must do to experience God's love. It is a picture of us pursuing our own pleasures in life, and not necessarily hating God, but just ignoring Him. The word repent in this context means to turn.

"Repent then, and turn to God,---"

THE PERFECT TREASURE

How can we experience God's love if we have our back to Him and are walking away? How can we experience God's love if we take no interest in Him? How can we experience God's love if we have no interest in pursuing Him? Our ears are positioned on our head in such a way that it is difficult to hear someone if we have our backs to them. Yes, God does love everyone on the face of this earth, but many people miss out on His love because they have their backs to Him and are walking away.

God created the human race so He would have someone to love. He created each human being to become the object of His love. He created each one so He would have a focal point for His love. Without approaching God to experience His love would be like me sitting in the car, trying to get warm, when the source of heat is the bonfire. I can look at the fire, and I can understand that fire produces heat; but unless I approach the fire, it will never warm me. Unless I approach God, I will never experience His perfect love.

Look what the Bible tells us about His love for us. John 3:16 states:

"For God so loved the world ---"

God, being the source of love, created man and woman to be the object of His love. He had to have someone to love. He created us in His image so He would have someone to pour out His love upon. He loved the world. He didn't create a goldfish to be the object of his love, because a goldfish could not love Him back. A goldfish will acknowledge Him and obey Him but is unable to love Him back. God created all mankind (every one of us) to receive His perfect love.

There is someone who perfectly loves me. If I am hungry to be loved, why would I ever turn my back on God and walk away? If I am hungry to be loved, why would I ever ignore the only being in the universe who is capable of loving me in a perfect way?

Chapter 3

What Does the Treasure Look Like?

What does perfect love look like? The word love is used to describe many different emotions. In my first book Joy, A Hidden Treasure (in plain sight) I noted my love for peanut butter. What a wonderful creation from God and Jif. Some evenings, if Beverly doesn't prepare a desert, I will get up from the dinner table and make half a P & J sandwich. It tastes so wonderful. I love peanut butter.

Is that real love? No it isn't. To be real love the peanut butter would be required to love me back. I have requested that many times, and to this day it has remained painfully silent. The only response I get from peanut butter is weight gain.

I probably shouldn't admit it, but I love pain pills. Recently I had major surgery, and I ended up with a three month supply of pain pills. While I was only taking one a day in the end, it still made me feel wonderful. About an hour into a pill, the song "Everything Is beautiful, In Its Own Way" would always pop into my mind. I loved pain Pills, but I could never get them to love me back.

Love is a word that is used to explain our emotions in many different situations. I loved my third grade teacher. I love the view out our dining room window. I love warm water in my shower. I love many different things, but none of these love me back.

To understand real love, however, we have to find someone who will love us when we are unlovable. Perfect love is found when we are loved even when we are mean. Perfect love is found when we do things to destroy someone and they just smile and open their arms and give us a warm embrace.

True love can only come from someone who is the source of love. If I can only love when love is being poured out upon me, then I am not the source of love, I am only a sponge absorbing love. Perfect love can only come from the source of love and that source is God.

What does the perfect treasure look like?

Look what the Bible says about that perfect love. Romans 5:8 states:

"but God demonstrates His own love for us in this: While we were still sinners, Christ died for us."

While we were still enemies of God, while we were spitting in His face and belittling Him, He sent His Son to die on the cross to pay the penalty for my sins -- one of the most painful deaths concocted by man. God initially loved us when we were unlovable.

I cannot imagine doing that. I cannot imagine someone burning my house down, spitting in my face, killing my wife out of hatred towards me, and then sending one of my children to die in the electric chair so that person could be set free, especially if there is a chance that enemy would never apologize or show gratitude. I just do not have that much love in me towards an enemy. Yet, that is exactly what God did.

God loves us so much that He prepared a way for us to enter into His presence even while we were still sinners and still His enemies. He made that painful sacrifice knowing that, perhaps 95% (arbitrary percentage) of the world would never show gratitude or be thankful. He made that sacrifice knowing that most of His enemies would never even take note of what He had done.

God made that sacrifice because of His

WHAT DOES THE TREASURE LOOK LIKE?

enormous love towards all mankind. As a technicality, He had to make that sacrifice because He is love. As heat has to come from a bonfire (the source of heat), love has to come from God, because He is the source of love. "God is love." God has to provide a way for sinners (people He loves) to enter into His presence. Otherwise, who would He have to pour out His endless love upon?

What does real love look like? Jesus, the one who willingly died on the cross states it this way in John 15:13

"Greater love has no one than this, that he lay down his life for his friends."

We were of no value, whatsoever, to the kingdom of God when Jesus died for our sins. We were enemies, we were sinners, and we were against every good thing God stood for. Yet Jesus died for us anyway, even if only 5% of the people on earth would receive the gift

He offered. That is real love. That is what the source of love is willing to give.

Love poured out but not returned.

There is a story in the Bible to help us understand that God loves us even when He knows we may never accept His love. Jesus (God upon the earth) tells the story of a rich young man. This man was a good business man who knew how to make money and invest money. I'm sure he was highly respected in the community because he drove a camel draped in jewels. He owned a beautiful home and possibly a second home on a lake in northern Michigan. He probably didn't own a Harley but I'm sure he owned one of the noisiest donkeys in the community.

This rich young man owned everything he'd ever dreamed about. Then one day he came to his senses, possibly after throwing an extravagant party with only the elite of the community in attendance. Whatever he

WHAT DOES THE TREASURE LOOK LIKE?

was going through, he came to the conclusion that all the worldly treasures he had amassed did not bring him the love he was looking for.

He wanted to be loved, not because of his wealth and his toys, but because he was worthy to be loved. This rich young man wanted to spend eternity in the presence of his loving and caring God. He realized his toys on this earth and the respect of friends was not enough.

He had heard about Jesus, and after chasing Him down, ran towards Him, and fell at His feet. He asked Jesus, "What must I do to spend eternity in your presence and the presence of the loving Father (my paraphrase of Mark 10:17b)?" Jesus looked him in the eye and his heart broke because He knew the man was not willing to give up his wealth. This rich young man longed for eternity, but was unwilling to meet the condition Jesus would set before him. The real god that he worshipped was his money.

The Bible tells us that Jesus "loved" him and wanted the very best for Him. Thus He told the rich young man to sell everything he owned, give the money to the poor, and then come and follow Him. The man thought about it for a few moments and then turned his back on Jesus and walked away. This rich young man totally rejected the perfect love he so desperately longed for. Jesus knew that rejection would be the outcome, but the Bible tells us He "loved" him anyway.

Jesus loves us even when we reject Him. Jesus loves everyone even when He knows only 5% will receive that love. Jesus loved His enemies because Jesus, the Son of God, is the source of love. That is what real love looks like.

Real love will never leave us.

What does real love look like? Someone who perfectly loves us will never leave us. God said to Joshua as he lead an army into

WHAT DOES THE TREASURE LOOK LIKE?

the promised land against fortified cities and warriors who stood nine feet tall:

> ***"No one will be able to stand up against you all the days of your life. As I was with Moses, so will I be with you; I will never leave you nor forsake you." Joshua 1:5***

I'm sure Joshua had many reservations about taking an untested army up against proven warriors. He had very little training and thus could not fall back on a history of victories. So, it was like God put a hand on his shoulder, looked him in the eye and said, "Joshua, don't be afraid. As the All Powerful God, I am going with you. You will never be out of My sight. I love you and with Me at your side, your enemies do not have a chance."

Real love is always with us. It will never leave us. I never have to worry about His love being withdrawn from me, even when I don't quite measure up to His standards. As a source of love He will never withdraw His love from me. He is love. When you stand next to a bonfire the fire cannot withdraw its heat from you. When you stand in the presence of God He cannot withdraw His love.

Real love drives out fear.

What does real love look like?
I John 4:18 reads:

"---perfect love drives out fear-".

Many people fear God because they know they are not living up to His expectations (and never will this side of heaven). They fear His wrath. They fear that lightening bolts will come from His fingers and crush them whenever they do something wrong. Fear carries with it the expectation of judgment.

While He may punish us when we do something wrong, God is love and that punishment comes to us out of the perfect love He has for us. He does not want to see us destroy our lives. He desires for us is to

WHAT DOES THE TREASURE LOOK LIKE?

live an abundant life on this earth, and that will not happen if we disobey Him.

When we acknowledge His unconditional love, and begin to experience this satisfying love, we no longer fear Him. We maintain a high respect for Him and obey Him, but we are no longer terrified of this powerful God, because He loves us. Perfect love drives out fear.

So what does the treasure look like? What does perfect love look like? Perfect love is a love that is poured out upon an enemy even when there is a potential that it will be rejected by that enemy. Perfect love is a love that is willing to give up something of great worth for a friend, even to the extreme of dying for that friend.

Real love will never be withdrawn.

Real love is a love that will never be withdrawn from a friend, no matter how much they hurt you. Because of that enduring love, the author of Romans states in Romans 8:38-39:

> *"For I am convinced that neither death nor life, neither angels nor demons, neither present nor the future, nor any powers, neither height nor depth, nor anything else in all creation, will be able to separate us from the love of God that is in Christ Jesus our Lord."*

Nothing can ever separate us from the love of God. Nothing! George Matheson knew this love. He became blind at the age of eighteen, and his fiance broke off their engagement because of his blindness. At forty his caretaker/sister left him so she could get married. He felt alone and discouraged yet knew his God still loved him. He wrote the hymn 'O Lord That Will Not Let Me Go'. The first verse reveals his deep confidence in God's love towards him.

WHAT DOES THE TREASURE LOOK LIKE?

***'O love that will not let me go,
I rest my weary soul in thee;
I give thee back the life I owe,
That in thine ocean depths its flow
   may richer, fuller be."***

In George's mind, even though everyone who loved him on this earth had left him, (a feeling I hope I never have to experience), he knew deep in his heart that his God would never leave him or withdraw His love from him. That is a beautiful confidence and a beautiful love. "God is love".

Personally experiencing God's love.

I have shared with you a number of passages from God's Word that explain what God's perfect love looks like. They are very encouraging and enlightening, but at the same time, they are just words. I am able to understand their meaning, but sometimes words fail to touch my heart. Words can be factual and yet cold at the same time.

So allow me to share with you my

LOVE, A HIDDEN TREASURE

personal encounters with God's love. To do so, I am going to relate it to something that happened to me when I was six years old. This is a feeble attempt to draw a picture of God's love, but this memory raises the same emotions I experience in God's presence.

I was at my grandfather's farm in northern Michigan, one of my favorite places on this earth. I have always loved his farm, because it is in the wilderness. It is eighty acres, carved out of six square miles of a national forest. I always felt like I was a frontier explorer when I went there. The day was a beautiful sunny day, and the fresh smell of northern Michigan was all around.

I was there with my mom and dad and two brothers. We were preparing to leave the farm to watch a parade in a neighboring town. I was excited about the parade, plus I knew dad would buy us ice cream cones because he loved ice cream so much.

As I look back, I realize I was

WHAT DOES THE TREASURE LOOK LIKE?

experiencing a perfect peace in my heart. The place was beautiful, and the event was going to be exciting. My mom and dad loved me, and I felt safe and secure in their presence. I did not know of any world events that would cause me fear, and there was a lot of laughter and joy all around me.

I had food to eat and a roof over my head. It was one of the most beautiful days I have ever experienced. At six years of age I did not have all those emotions flowing through me, but, as I look back, I do remember how special that day was. I was loved. I was protected, and I was cared for. I was experiencing a warm and perfect peace. Life was simple and beautiful.

That is what God's perfect love looks like. It brings us perfect peace and complete safety. It is a place that is bright and joyful no matter what is going on around us. While experiencing God's love, life just seems to be more simple, with very few complications attached.

As I spend time in prayer I am able to experience those emotions, if only for a few seconds at a time. At six years of age, grandpa's farm took my eyes off of earthly problems, hurts, aches, and pains (which seem to be mounting as I get older). God's love is like experiencing that simple but beautiful day.

It taught me that when I take time to enter into God's love, my being experiences a perfect peace, and I go to a place where there are no troubles. My life becomes simple and yet complete. That is the best way I can explain God's perfect love. It is a beautiful experience even if it only lasts for a few seconds at a time.

How do we find this love? Is there a treasure map to help us find our way? Yes there is. But few will ever discover the map, and fewer yet will ever begin the journey. Isn't that sad? Love is the most precious treasure sought after, and the map is so clear. Yet for some, the cost is too great. Will you proceed from here, or are you one who will have nothing to do with any further instructions?

Chapter #4
The Treasure Map
Part 1

It is almost impossible to find a treasure without a treasure map, but sometimes the treasure map can even be confusing because of misunderstood directions. In the 50's, the Mickey Mouse Club TV show (yes, I am that old) had a series called the Hardy Boys. In this series a treasure of gold doubloons and pieces of eight were hidden someplace in the community.

A treasure map was discovered saying that the treasure was hidden in the tower in the wall by the stairs. The whole city turned

LOVE, A HIDDEN TREASURE

out as the owners of the map began to tear the walls apart on the three story tower on old Mr. Applegate's estate. The walls by the stairs were ripped open one floor at a time. But alas there was no treasure.

Sometime later the treasure was discovered, by accident, near the stairs, in the wall of the old water tower wall at the train station. The map was very clear. It was just misinterpreted. In the same way, the treasure map to love is also very clear. Yet most people misinterpret the map, if they read it at all. The problem with most people is that they have preconceived ideas on how to find love, and thus never discover that beautiful unconditional love God has for them.

The Bible tells us that God is love. Therefore, to be loved and to understand love we must know God. The Bible does not say it is good enough to know about God, but, that we must know Him. It is the same with a bonfire. We can know all the facts about a bonfire, but we never truly experience heat and warmth until we approach the bonfire. Then the closer we get, the warmer we get. So the treasure map to love is to know God. 1 John 4:8 tells us:

> ***"Whoever does not love does not know God because God is love."***

God is love. Love is the very essence of His very being. Love is as vital a part of God as a heart is to a human being. You cannot separate a heart from a human being and still have a live human being. In the same way you cannot separate love from God and still have God. So the treasure map to love is very simple --- to know God. Yet many people take it upon themselves to interpret what it means to know God. You must know God.

Some people feel they can move close to God and be pleasing to God by going to the right church. I challenge you to reference, from the Bible, what denomination that would be? I am a retired Wesleyan pastor and while the Wesleyan Church is a Bible centered church it is never mentioned in the Bible. The two denominations mentioned are the Baptist (John the Baptist) and the Nazarene (Jesus the Nazarene). But neither are mentioned as denominations but simply to identify people.

The Wesleyan, Baptist, Nazarene, Catholic, Lutheran, and Congregational Church will never be able to guarantee you a relationship with God. You cannot attend any denomination and be guaranteed a relationship with God. You must personally know God. Nor does attending church guarantee that you are a good person and that you find favor with God. You must know God.

We don't know God by doing good deeds.

Some people are sure that they can

approach God by doing a lot of good deeds --more good deeds than bad deeds. Sorry, but that is ridiculous. Let's say you do 2,000,002 bad deeds in your lifetime and 2,000,003 good deeds. Are you so naive to think that will bring you closer to God and allow you to enter into His love? Basically, you are still a very bad person -- 2,000,002 deeds worth of bad.

You don't know God by giving money.

Some people feel they can get close to God and experience His love by giving money to charities. That is a wonderful and kind-hearted thing to do and an act that will benefit many. It is an act that will even bless the giver. But if giving money is done to grow close to God, then how will the very poor be able to get to know Him? Man's conceived ways of getting close to God are fruitless.

Here is the Map!

There is a way of entering into God's presence and experiencing God's love, but it

LOVE, A HIDDEN TREASURE

is not an avenue created by man. There is a way to know God and enjoy His love, but you cannot reinterpret the treasure map to get there. You must follow the map step by step and the Bible contains the only map.

In Matthew 7:13-14 Jesus draws this word picture as He talks to the crowd.

"--- Enter through the narrow gate. For wide is gate and broad is the road that leads to destruction, and many enter through it. But small is the gate and narrow the road that leads to life, and only a few find it."

Jesus is illustrating the first step we must take to enter into God's presence to experience His love. We must enter through the narrow gate that leads to life.

This is a picture of people walking down a very wide avenue. They are simply enjoying life and enjoying the things this world has

THE TREASURE MAP - PART 1

to offer. Some have their arms around each other. Some are bent on having successful careers, some are simply talking on their cell phones. Some are excited about their next purchase. While others are excited about their new found friend. Whatever story each traveler has, they are all enjoying life to the best of their ability.

At the end of the wide avenue is a wide gate that leads toward destruction, and most will go through it unless an earlier decision is made. People seldom consider the wide gate (the end of their life on this earth) but simply pass through it by default.

But, along that wide avenue, off to one side is a narrow gate. It is not all that attractive. There is grass growing up in the path to the gate because few have traveled it. The gate is overgrown with vines and seems to be unattended. Very few people on the wide avenue will even notice that gate, and still fewer will enter through it.

LOVE, A HIDDEN TREASURE

In this picture, the narrow gate represents Jesus. To the people journeying through this world, Jesus is not all that attractive. He seems to be too restrictive, too judgmental, and according to the politically correct people, too hateful. So, of the few who will look His way, even fewer will walk His way, even though He is the one who leads to life.

Jesus is the narrow gate.

According to this passage, Jesus is the narrow gate and the pathway to God. Other scriptures supports this same truth. In John 14:6 Jesus states:

"---I am the way and the truth and the life. No one comes to the Father except through Me."

Jesus makes it very clear. Without Him you will never see God and never experience His love. The reason for this will be explained later.

THE TREASURE MAP - PART 1

In Acts 4:12 Luke states:

"Salvation is found in none else, for there is no other name under heaven given to men by which we must be saved."

In previous verses Luke is referring to Jesus. In other words, no one will experience God's love. No one will get to heaven, and no one will be saved except through Jesus. Jesus is the narrow gate that leads to life.

It is so fascinating that Jesus, the narrow gate, is so unattractive to the world, yet the life we experience after we pass through that gate is so amazing. I will expand on that exciting journey in chapter seven, but for now let us examine our journey towards the narrow gate.

The first step

The first step of our journey toward God is a little negative. It is a little bit of a "downer" to the human race. Many feel that the more intelligent we become the better off the human race will be. But the Bible tells us that is not true. In fact the Bible tells us that we are not very good people, and that is a hard fact for many to swallow. Romans 3:23 states that:

"---all have sinned and fall short of the glory of God."

We are sinners. We were born sinners, and unless we take the proper steps we will die sinners. We are more prone to do evil deeds than good deeds. We are more apt to participate in deeds that benefit ourselves than deeds that are of greater benefit to others. So here we are a sinful people trying to get close to a perfectly Holy God, and it will simply never happen. In fact just the opposite is true. Romans 6:23

"For the wages of sin is death--------"

The death mentioned here is interpreted, "separation from God". So instead of entering into God's presence, we separate ourselves from God. It's pretty hard to experience love, when we separate ourselves further and further from the source of love.

It is only logical that sin seperates us from the God of love. As a sinner, I concentrate on the sin more than I concentrate on God. If gambling is my sin, then my every thought is on the next draw of the cards or the next lottery ticket. I witness people buying tickets at the gas station and before they start their engines they are compelled to scratch the ticket to see if they have won. It's an adrenalin rush. The next win is what they concentrate on, not God.

If drugs become our sin, it is hard to even think about God when our every thought is where to purchase the next high. If sex is our sin, it is hard to experience excitement in God when our greater pleasure and pasttime is found in sex. If gossip is our sin, it is hard to get close to God when we concentrate so hard on receiving and sharing inappropriate information with anyone who will listen.

As distance separates us from the heat of a bonfire, so our sin separates us from the love of God. In order to approach God and experience His love, we must do something to eliminate our sin. Unfortunately, that is impossible for us to do. The more we concentrate on overcoming the sin, the more we concentrate on the sin. The more we concentrate on the sin, the more we sin. Thus, we find ourselves in a desperate situation.

We cannot create our own path to God.

So what can we do to have a relationship with God and enter into His perfect love? We cannot! It is impossible for a sinful person to do anything to get closer to God. But God is willing to break through the sin barrier from His side. He loves us so much that He made

THE TREASURE MAP - PART 1

an unbelievable sacrifice to allow us to enter into His presence. Romans 5:8 tells us of His love.

"But God demonstrates His own love for us in this: While we were still sinners, Christ died for us."

Jesus, God's perfect son, paid the penalty for our sins. When He died on the cross, the sins of the world past, present, and future were heaped on Him. Our penalty for sin is separation from God both now and eternally, but Jesus paid the penalty for those sins. He paid our penalty. Now we no longer have to pay that penalty. Now, we no longer have to be separated from God. We no longer have to be separated from that beautiful and satisfying unconditional love.

My part in God's plan.

But, you ask, isn't there something we have to do? Yes there is and the answer

LOVE, A HIDDEN TREASURE

is simple. We either accept, by faith, the wonderful knowledge that Jesus died for our sins and paid the penalty for our sins, or we reject it by not taking the next step. God tells us in John 1:12

> ***"Yet to all who received Him, to those who believe in His name, He gave the right to become children of God---"***

There are two key words in this verse, to "receive" Him and to "believe" in His name. To receive Him we have to say, "Jesus, I am a sinner. You paid the penalty for my sins and I ask that you forgive me of my sins. I receive that wonderful gift and now I ask that you come and dwell in my heart. I openly receive you as my Savior for you have saved me from the wide gate that leads to destruction". That is what receiving looks like.

Then we have to believe in His name. If He is to become my Savior, then I have to believe what He says. I have to believe His every word. I can no longer pick and choose what I want to believe. If you believe me, and I tell you that as you go to the grocery store this evening, a semi will hit you going seventy miles per hour and you will be killed, then you will likely not leave the house --- if you believe me. In the same way, if you believe Jesus, you will listen to Him (through His Word) and do what He says. You will accept what He says as truth and hunger for every word that He speaks, because you know it will bring you a far better life.

Obey, Obey, Obey

In an earlier book, ***Joy, A Hidden Treasure (in plain sight)***, I mentioned that obedience was the one thing that kept me from becoming a Christian until I was thirty one years old. I did not want to obey His every word because I did not want to be tied down to a bunch of oppressing rules. I

LOVE, A HIDDEN TREASURE

wanted to be free and do what I thought was fun. But then as I began my spiritual journey, I realized every rule Jesus gave me had His love written all over it.

As parents we had rules for our children, and I'm sure they thought our rules were oppressive. They couldn't ride their bikes on a busy highway because they could be killed. When they were teens, we tried to enforce curfews because we wanted our children to be safe and get good grades. We didn't have rules to oppress them and make their lives miserable. We had rules because we loved them and knew a whole lot more about life than they did. It was our love that caused us to set boundaries for our children.

In the same way, God knows a whole lot more about life than we know. We don't know what the next second will bring. He sees our whole future. We fail to see the hurt our sins will cause us. We only see the momentary pleasure. God sees how each sin will destroy the quality of life He wants us to have, and He says, "Do not do that. I love you way too much to see you experience devastation in your life". So to believe God means that you believe Jesus paid the penalty for your sin and that every word He utters has love written all over it. Thus we benefit ourselves when we obey Him.

These are the first steps we must take to know God and have a close relationship with Him. We must confess that we are really not good people, and that we are sinners.

Then we must accept the fact that our sins separate us from God. They do not bring us closer so we can experience His love, they separate us. Next we must ask God to forgive us our sins and ask Jesus to come and dwell in our heart and be Lord of our life. We must receive Him and then believe every word He utters. Then and only then will we begin to experience His love, His good and pleasing and perfect love.

These are the steps we must take if we desire to go through the narrow gate that leads to life. These are the steps we must take if we desire to enter into God's presence and experience His wonderful love. Is the experience worth the effort? It doesn't look like it from the perspective of the wide avenue. In fact it looks rather unpleasing. It looks like we have to turn our backs on all the things we enjoy in the world. Just the opposite is true, however. When we go through the narrow gate, good things happen.

In chapter 7 we will look at what happens to our life as we pass through the narrow gate, but first, lets look at the second and third part of the treasure map. Some Christians just take the first step and complain that the Christian life is boring. Why does that happen? It happens because there is a second and third part of the treasure map that has been ignored. Ignore these next two steps and you will become one bored Christian.

Chapter 5
The Treasure Map
Part 2

We know that to experience God's heart warming love we must enter through the "narrow gate". We must ask God to forgive us our sins (all our bad deeds) and invite Jesus to be Lord of our life. There is no other way for a sinful person to enter into the presence of a perfectly holy God. Our sins must be terribly repulsive to God.

I was on a trip with a group of men. One of the guys didn't shower for two days and it was very warm. The odor was so bad I had to get up and walk away. That must be what God feels when we try to enter His presence without our sins forgiven. That is something that will simply never happen. We will never experience His unconditional love as an unforgiven human being. Picture Him getting up and walking away as you approach Him as a sinner. He must smell the stench of our sins. What a terrifying experience!

Yet, after that first step, after we enter through the narrow gate, we must continue on our journey by taking a second step. We must look at part two of the treasure map. Some Christians ask Jesus to be Lord of their life and remain at that level of spiritual maturity for the rest of their lives. That is not a good decision to make. That is like a baby being born and then being abandoned to grow into adulthood alone. It will simply never happen. We all know that a baby is helpless, and if left alone he will die.

We must join a fellowship of believers.

So what is the second part of the

THE TREASURE MAP - PART 2

treasure map? It is simply this; we must grow spiritually. We must grow and understand more about this wonderful God, so we can learn to love Him even more. Our journey has just begun. We must understand how beautiful our new Lord and God really is, and that means joining a fellowship of believers. We must surround ourselves with people who are able to teach us and encourage us. Hebrews 10:25 states it this way:

"And let us not give up meeting together, as some are in the habit of doing, but let us encourage one another - and all the more as you see the Day approaching"

There is no such thing as a "Lone Ranger Christian". A baby Christian cannot go it on their own. There must be encouragement, Bible study, and lessons in truth. We need to hear the good and bad experiences others

LOVE, A HIDDEN TREASURE

have had, learn from them, and be encouraged by them. We must have Christians around us to encourage us and pray for us. We need to be around other people of like minds.

Growing through the experience of others.

Let me give you an example of older Christians encouraging others. This is an example I used in my first book but it is so huge in my life I will share it again. The day we announced to my family that we were going into the ministry was the day we realized our three year old son had lost total sight in his right eye.

You talk about a slap in the face from God. We were doing God such a favor and He allows this tragedy to happen? Plus, as a father who does not want anything bad to ever happen to one of my children, I will fight back. The next Sunday we took our son to the front of the church to be prayed over. God failed to answer our prayers. At thirty five our son is still blind in his right eye. God failed to answer our prayer---or did He?

In his teens John was an outfielder for our church softball team, and he was one of our best outfielders. He was fast and had total depth perception. A person with one eye cannot have depth perception. You need two eyes to measure distance. Had God answered that prayer twelve years earlier? Yes He did. He just answered in a different way than we prayed. John even played goalie on a college soccer team. The balls came at him seventy mph from ten feet away. John was a good goalie because he had depth perception.

Too often we pray for God to accommodate our needs and when He doesn't answer we may feel He is off playing golf somewhere. We feel He doesn't listen or doesn't care or maybe doesn't even answer prayers anymore. Yet I am here to encourage you that God, who loves us so completely, answers every prayer you pray. It is just that sometimes His answer

LOVE, A HIDDEN TREASURE

is different than you ask, or sometimes He waits for His perfect timing.

If you are trying to worship God away from the church, you may never hear encouraging stories like this. You may never hear encouraging lessons from His Holy Word. You may never learn the beautiful lessons of grace as you have to worship with imperfect people. It's true, the church is not perfect, but it must be your uppermost priority if you are to grow spiritually, and it is imperative that you grow spiritually.

Attending a body of believers is not an option if you desire to grow and experience more and more of God's warm and unconditional love. We can learn so much from each other and encourage one another as we grow.

One more illustration to show the importance of finding and attending a Bible teaching church. A young man wanted to learn karate to defend himself, and there was

THE TREASURE MAP - PART 2

a major, "winner take all" karate tournament twenty years down the road. The young man signed up for the lessons. He joined the class but never attended the first lesson.

Over the next twenty years he made up his own karate moves. He invented the head butt leading with his nose. He could only practice this move once a week, however, because it gave him such a bad nose bleed. He perfected the back flip kicking his opponent in the little finger on the way over. He even created the free fall, hitting his opponent in the big toe on the way down. Ridiculous? Yes! Yet so are some of the things we believe about God if we are not participating in a fellowship of believers.

This young man rigorously prepared himself for the "winner take all" tournament. Finally the tournament arrived. He had no clue what real karate moves looked like and so when he got into his first match he lost in the first three seconds. He didn't even have time to use one of his moves he had practiced and perfected over the past twenty years.

I will admit this is a ridiculous example but it is no more ridiculous than someone becoming a Christian and then making up his own rules along the way on what God is like and how to get to heaven. The Bible is very clear. Jesus is the only way. In order to know His ways we must be a part of a Bible believing church. To learn to love unlovable people we must be a part of a Bible-believing church. To learn the path to eternal life we must be a part of a Bible-believing church.

These are the first two steps of entering into and experiencing God's perfect, heartwarming and unconditional love. There can be no substitution for these first two steps, but the third part of the treasure map has a number of variables in it. Remember the goal is to approach God, to get closer and closer to Him, and to experience the only unconditional, satisfying love on the face of their earth, because God is the only source of love. God is love.

Chapter 6
The Treasure Map
Part 3

There are variables in the third part of the treasure map because every person entering through the narrow gate has a totally different personality. We all relate to things in different ways. When I was a boy I remember the sounds of crows back in the woods. The sound was so soothing to me. When I hear crows today it is a very relaxing sound. Yet to my wife it is an ugly screeching sound.

We are all so different and thus there are many variations of getting close to God in this third step. Some try to worship God in a style that does not fit their personality, and they easily become bored. They may feel church is boring and dull. They may even feel God is boring and dull because they are trying to get close to Him by using a method someone else swears by.

Gary Thomas in his book ***Sacred Pathways*** noticed some were forced into a worship style that didn't fit their personality. He began to wonder, "If God intentionally make us all different, why should everyone be expected to love God in the same way?" After some study he realized that over the years, man has worshipped God in many different ways. As you read on, see if one of these styles of worship best fits your personality. If you worship God in the style that fits you best, you will grow closer to God and experience more of His love.

Gary identifies nine of the ways people draw close to God and then I will add a couple at the end. Here are Gary's nine.

The ***naturalist*** is most inspired to worship God in the out of doors, possibly listening to the beautiful, comforting sound of a crow or simply feeling close in His creation. They may hear the orchestra of birds at a sunrise and realize that God is a glorious being. They may witness the silence in the woods in the dead of winter and feel ever so close to God. The weakness of the naturalist is they may feel the out of doors is their church and never grow in "truth" from God's Holy Word.

The ***sensates*** love God with their senses. They appreciate beautiful worship services that involve their sight, taste, smell, and touch, not just their ears. The music may cause them to want to dance or clap their hands or lift their hands toward heaven. A perfumed censer may draw their very being into the heart of a beautiful God. Hugging a person next to them may make them sense an earthly version of God's love. The problem is that the sensate may not feel these senses in every service and thus, may go home feeling God didn't show up on a given Sunday morning.

The ***Traditionalists*** draw closer to God through rituals, liturgies, symbols, and unchanging structure. A friend of mine relates to God in this way. As he travels he can attend any church within his denomination, any place in the country and always feel right at home. There are simply no surprises. The surrounding is always much the same. Thus, he will never feel uncomfortable or out of place.

The ***Ascetics*** prefer to worship God in solitude and simplicity. The things the traditionalist prefer are simply a distraction in creating a oneness with God. This would be one of my favorite styles. As a pastor, I simply had to get away from the church, the people, and the administrative responsibilities to be at one with God. Even my Bible study at the church was directed more at developing

THE TREASURE MAP - PART 3

a sermon than for my personal benefit and growth.

The ***Activists*** love God through confronting evil, battling injustice, and working to make the world a better place. They feel close to God when they are allowed to defend the Kingdom. They feel close to God when they do what they feel Jesus would do if He were still on this earth.

Caregivers feel close to God by loving others and meeting their needs. This group might include a Hospice worker or someone who takes care of an aging parent. They may have trouble with their siblings, because they will not come along side and care for their loved one. They may feel their siblings have no compassion and are cold hearted, when all along they are simply gifted in another area.

Enthusiasts love God through celebration. They feel close to God when they can express themselves openly. They love encouraging messages and pep rally type services. They may tend toward TV evangelists who may become quite emotional and excitable.

Contemplatives love God through adoration. They may feel close to God when they are allowed to pour out their praises at the feet of Jesus. They would be more apt to concentrate on the more positive aspects of Jesus, delighting themselves in His glory, His strength, and His beauty.

Intellectuals love God by studying with their minds. They would be more apt to be the preachers or the theologians. They feel close to God by trying to understand His mind and then help others understand it.

I will personally add another way some feel close to God. Those who ***Memorize*** scripture feel they are hiding the very mind and thoughts of God in their heart. They feel close to God because they are able to recall numerous passages when needed without taking time to hunt them up. They have

THE TREASURE MAP - PART 3

memorized many of God's thoughts and thus are able to live closer to God. The more they memorize the closer they feel.

And yet others feel close to God by spending extended time each day in *prayer*. A person with this type of personality is able to talk some and listen much. Prayer time is not just pouring out your heart to God. It is also listening for His direction and wisdom. I have never personally heard God's voice, but while in the listening part of prayer, some wonderful thoughts and insights have entered my mind.

These are eleven ways to enter into God's presence and thus experience more of His love. It is so refreshing to be able to do it our way, the way God personally created us to individually worship Him, and feel close to Him. As a new Christian I had a number of people tell me that unless I do "such and such" as they were doing, I must not love God.

They made me feel very guilty. They

LOVE, A HIDDEN TREASURE

made me feel I could only enter God's presence one way. At first that was very confusing.

I am so thankful God has allowed me to enter into His presence and experience His love in increasing proportion through solitary moments, extended prayer, memorization, and studying His Word. But, just because I am blessed in these four ways does not mean anyone else has to copy me. In fact I will encourage you to become aware of the ways God is personally calling you into His presence. When you do, your relationship will grow and you will be able to experience a greater share of His unconditional love.

Chapter 7
The Treasure Beyond The Narrow Gate

As mentioned earlier, on the "wide avenue" side of the narrow gate, the path is overgrown with grass, vines are growing wild, and the gate may even need a little paint. Few people are leaving the wide avenue to investigate this "out of the way" gate. The narrow gate represents Jesus, and walking with Jesus is just not attractive as we walk in this world. He asked the rich young man to give all his money to the poor and come and follow Him. He asked Peter to give up his profession, his only source of income, and come and follow Him.

LOVE, A HIDDEN TREASURE

Jesus, the narrow gate, even commands us to love our enemies, when we would rather hold a grudge and wish them bad karma. He asks that if someone steals our push lawn mower, we go buy a brand new "0" turn riding mower, and give it to them. He tells us, if we are even angry with another person, it's like committing murder and that's a life sentence. Jesus, the narrow gate, does not look attractive from the wide road (from the worldly point of view) and thus very few people enter through that gate and very few people will ever experience God's beautiful unconditional love.

But what is life really like on the other side of that unkept narrow gate? What is life like when we ask God to forgive us our sins and ask Jesus to be Lord of our life? Life becomes a whole lot more exciting than most people can ever imagine.

The first thing we experience through the narrow gate is God's unconditional love.

This beautiful love is the most gratifying and fulfilling love we will ever know. As mentioned before, the love was always there, we just had our backs turned to it. But all of a sudden we sense that the God who should judge us the harshest, is the God who loves us the most. The God that we feared the most is now the God who pours out the most love upon us.

I live with a disease in my fingers called duputrens contractions. After one operation the doctor suggested a therapy of dipping my hand in warm oil. The warm oil therapy was very soothing, relaxing and comforting and it took some of the pain away. It was amazing.

When I think back on my conversion, that is the best way I can describe God's love being poured out upon me. It was soothing, relaxing, comforting, and it took some of my pain away. It was like warm oil being poured over my head and comforting my whole being. God's love towards me is amazing.

LOVE, A HIDDEN TREASURE

Joy is another experience we sense going through the narrow gate, and the further we travel the more joy we discover. We make ourselves familiar with God's promises and begin to realize how wonderful life on this earth can become. His promises are so comforting.

Promises like:

Romans 8:28 "And we know that in all things God works for the good for those who love Him,---"

John 16:24 "Until now you have not asked for anything in My name. Ask and you will receive, and your joy will be complete."

Joshua 1:5 "---I will never leave you nor forsake you."

***Joshua 1:8** "Do not let this book of the law depart from your mouth; meditate on it day and night, so you may be careful to do everything written It. Then you will be prosperous and successful."*

***Romans 6:23** "---but the gift of God is eternal life in Christ Jesus our Lord."*

All of these promises bring joy to my heart even as I go through difficult times. Life is good on the other side of the narrow gate. It just seems to open up a bright and beautiful life.

As I mentioned in an earlier book, ***Joy, A Hidden Treasure(in plain sight)*** we also discover peace on the other side of the narrow gate. It is not a peace that comes, because we never experience another difficulty. It is a peace in the midst of difficulty. It is a peace that comes because we begin to agree with the all powerful God instead of arguing with Him. It is a peace that comes because we have stopped trying to rewrite His book to make it fit our life style. We just accept it as truth and learn from it.

Paul said it best in his book to the church at Philippi in Philippians 4:6-7

"Do not be anxious about anything, but in everything, by prayer and petition, with thanksgiving, present your requests to God.and the peace of God, which transcends all understanding, will guard your hearts and your minds in Christ Jesus."

When we become anxious about the events in our life, we lose our peace. But God has the above plan to bring it back. A deep inner peace is discovered on the other side of the narrow gate.

The first three discoveries on the other side of the narrow gate have been exciting to me, but, this next one has been a struggle. Patience! As I grow older I am experiencing more patience, but perhaps I am only 20% of the way there. Why do I always pick the longest line in the grocery store? Why, in a restaurant, do people who come in after me receive their food before me? And why, in a doctor's office, do I announce loudly to the receptionist that the doctor said if I come right in I can go ahead of everyone (and that makes some heads turn) and then see the doctor two hours and forty-five minutes later. Of course, the first thing the nurse does is take my blood pressure, and naturally it is higher than normal.

The gift of patience needs a lot more growth within me, but I am becoming more aware of my lack of patience. I am becoming aware of how critical I become and how that gift of criticism makes those I love

LOVE, A HIDDEN TREASURE

feel uneasy around me. Thank you God for making me aware of my criticism, so I can comfort those I love instead of stirring them up. Thank you for the patience you are teaching me.

These are just a few of the things we experience beyond the narrow gate. It's like a light is turned on, and we can begin to see the more valuable things life has to offer. Once we see the valuable things, the things that bring us only momentary pleasure become less important.

But what about God's wrath?

In this book, I have portrayed God as being a God of love, a God being the very source of love. He is a God who loves you because He is love. Yet all through the writing I have sidestepped the fact that the Bible tells us that God can be a God of wrath. He can be very upset at times. So, am I leading people on, just sharing the wonderful and beautiful characteristics of God? As a salesman, am I just sharing with you how great a pill can be without spending five minutes telling you about all the side effects?

A. W. Tozer, in his book, ***Man: The Dwelling Place of God*** offers the best explanation I have heard defining God's wrath. His explanation is beautiful and turns a negative word like wrath into something beautiful. Plus, it makes God's love even more exciting.

God's Word speaks about His wrath around three hundred different times, so it is something that cannot be overlooked in this book about love. Yes, God is love but He is also a God of wrath in certain circumstances. But, as Tozer so beautifully points out, His anger is as holy as His love and the two are totally compatible.

You see, God is completely holy and has made holiness to be a moral condition necessary to the health of His children. Sin's temporary presence in our life robs us of our moral health. Whatever is holy is healthy, while evil is a moral sickness that leads to death (the definition of a life separated from God).

Since God's first concern for His children is moral health, that is holiness, whatever destroys that health is what causes Him to be angry---real angry. Where ever holiness confronts sin, there is a conflict. To preserve His people God must destroy whatever destroys them. When He arises to deal with the destruction of His people He is said to be angry.

God's wrath is His utter intolerance of whatever hurts or destroys His first love, His people. He hates sin as much as a mother hates cancer in a child or anything that would destroy the life of her child. God's wrath is Him simply saying, "I love you so much that I cannot tolerate the sin in your life that is destroying you. Separate yourself from the evil I hate before it destroys your life and I send judgment upon you.".

Wow! God's wrath is just another sign of how much He loves us. It is a sign that God desires a fulfilling and joyful life for us as we walk on this earth. So in my eyes, His wrath is just further proof of His tremendous love for me. As a parent disciplines their child to protect them from destroying their life, so God disciplines us to keep us from destroying our life. Now that is love.

Life is good on the other side of the narrow gate. Life is good when we begin our journey with Jesus.

LOVE, A HIDDEN TREASURE

Chapter 8
Guarding The Treasure

When I became a Christian, my life took an amazing turn for the good. Even when bad things happened to me, life seemed to be better because I was better equipped to handle them. Little things began to happen in my life. People laughed at me when I told them that the grass seemed greener. All of a sudden it became a richer green even though it was the same color.

Early in my working career I was designing vacation homes in northern Michigan for people we called "down-staters". Many of those down-staters

LOVE, A HIDDEN TREASURE

came from the Detroit area, an area of car factories, foundries, and machine shops. I can remember then saying, in amazement, how blue the sky was in northern Michigan. It was beautiful, especially as you looked at it through the green pine trees. They were right.

Yet, as I made that commitment to follow Christ, the northern Michigan sky became even bluer to me. My life changed drastically in the next few years. Even though I was far from perfect, I sensed I was experiencing a wonderful life. I couldn't define it at the time, but as I look back, I know I was beginning to sense God's love being poured out on me. As He poured it out, everyday things just became more beautiful.

Those early days of my new life were pleasing and exciting. Everything seemed to work out in a positive way. I had one account in Detroit that was a three store chain. I wrote a lot of business with them. But I knew the history of my product well enough to know that if they would give me more shelf space (buy more variety) I could make that chain a lot more money. Sales history proved that my product would make them more money per lineal foot of shelf space than any other product in their store. The store owners would just not listen. At one meeting I was so upset I slammed my sales book closed, got up, and walked out of the store (that was pre Jesus days). Needless to say, that move did not improve my sales with them.

Then one year later, as Jesus began to change my life, I went back into that store and somehow, felt a more positive emotion toward them. Unfortunately I didn't apologize, and my sales with them did not go up; but I was excited to be around the owners and store managers. It didn't matter how much I sold them, I just enjoyed their presence. I began to esteem them as gifted businessmen. Life just seemed better after I began to walk with

LOVE, A HIDDEN TREASURE

Jesus as my Savior.

I remember hiking by myself in the beautiful woods of northern Michigan one day in my early days with Jesus, and I began to realize how fortunate I was to be married to my beautiful wife. Beverly was raised on a farm and is a wonderful cook. She was very content to be a stay-at-home mom and take care of our family. That was important because at that time in my life I was traveling a lot.

All of these thoughts towards her began to overwhelm me. So as I walked, out of gratitude for what God had given me, I began to pray, "God, help me to love my wife more. Help me become a husband who will make her feel more complete." I don't remember an immediate response but within the next six months she became even more attractive to me.

Those early years with Jesus were so special. As I turned and faced Him, and began to walk toward Him, He just poured out more and more of His love upon me. As He did, my life took a wonderful turn for the better.

Then, as the years passed, even though His love for me never waned, I began to sense it less and less. Possibly I just became immune to His love and thus the contrast between my old life and new life became less intense. Possibly.

During those early years I was a sponge, absorbing all the good things (love) I could from the exciting God I had just began to serve. My life was amazing and even though I began to face many trials, everything seemed to begin going my way.

Yet, as I began to grow spiritually those emotions began to wane. God's love was still there in all its glory, I just seemed to sense it less. The problem was, I had become a sponge, absorbing God's love and not giving a whole lot away. One of my friends urged me

LOVE, A HIDDEN TREASURE

to stop talking so much about what God was doing for me (I was boring him to death) and start talking about what I was doing for God.

I was becoming like the Salt Sea in the Middle East. The Jordan river runs into the Salt Sea and since it is the lowest land elevation on the face of the earth nothing flows out. Everything that flows into the sea stays there. It is a stagnant body of water and is also referred to as the dead sea because there is very little aquatic life in the sea. It is just too stagnant and too full of chemicals. Over the centuries the Salt Sea has become nine times saltier than the ocean.

I was becoming like the salt sea. All of God's love was flowing in and very little was flowing out. The entirety of God's love was flowing in, and I was just holding on to it, with intensity. I had never been loved like that before. I don't think I had ever sensed being loved that perfectly, even though I was doing nothing to earn it.

GUARDING THE TREASURE

Why did it mean so much at first and so much less a little later? At first I was in dire need of that perfect love. But, after absorbing so much I didn't have room for any more. I was like a water pitcher being filled with water. After it is filled to the rim you can not force any more water into it. Any water poured into the pitcher after that will simply spill out and be wasted.

The same is true with God's precious love. At first, my heart needed to be filled with His precious love. But once it was filled, any extra was just not usable. I could only take in so much love at a time. If I wanted more I had to give some away.

John makes this clear in I John 4:10-11 when he states:

"Dear friends, since God so loved us so, we ought to love one another. No one has ever seen God; but if we love one another, God lives in us and His love is made complete in us."

LOVE, A HIDDEN TREASURE

When we love one another, the invisible God reveals Himself to others through us, and His love is made complete because it is flowing through us and touching others. When it does that, when I have given some of God's love away by loving others, I have made room within to receive another quantity of love from Him.

It is made complete because I have allowed His love to flow through me and touch others. Jesus is no longer on this earth, in a physical form, to touch and love people like He loved the twelve disciples. He is no longer here to encourage people as He did Peter and others as they made blundering mistakes. He is not here to comfort and forgive those caught in adultery. Jesus is no longer here to feed five thousand hungry people stranded on a mountainside. He is no longer here to reveal His love to those He created to love. The only channel for His love today is me.

When I love others, two dynamic events

GUARDING THE TREASURE

take place. First His love flows through me to touch others, and thus others witness God's unconditional love. Second, I have given away some of His love so I have room to receive a fresh quantity of His heart warming love myself. I have to stop here and make the following observation. "Life just doesn't get any better than that."

How do I guard the love God gives to me? I guard it by giving it away. I guard it by giving it away to every life I touch on the face of this earth. And the more I give away the more of His new and amazing love I receive. Will I ever use up all the love God has to give? That is impossible. His love is endless. I do not have to hoard it. I am blessed with more of His love, only if I am willing to share more with others. That is how I guard the treasure.

LOVE, A HIDDEN TREASURE

Chapter 9
Sharing The Treasure

This will be a fairly short chapter as the method for sharing God's love is not really complex. Many churches are compelling their people to go out and share God's love through witnessing. This is a wonderful exercise, and it is based on scripture. In Acts 1:8 Jesus tells His disciples that they are to be His witnesses, when the Holy Spirit comes upon them.

One of the problems with churches teaching their people to witness is that they teach using methods. My favorite method is something called the "Bridge Illustration".

Others enjoy using the "Romans Road", and yet others are taught different methods of witnessing. A very popular way to witness is called "Friendship Evangelism". Others draw people to Christ by planting churches. Some turn out well.

Methods Without Love Just Won't Work

All these methods have stories of success, though most are very limited after they run their course. Jesus told His disciples they will be His witnesses when the Holy Spirit comes upon them. The disciples prayed for that to happen over a period of ten days, and when the Holy Spirit did, indeed, come upon them, three thousand came to know Jesus in one day.

My point is this. What if churches taught people to live daily in the power of the Holy Spirit, not just praying for the Holy Spirit to heal their sick, or bring a friend to know Christ, or even for more money to pay bills. But, pray that the power of the Holy Spirit come upon them so they could become effective witnesses. That seemed to be Jesus' method.

Let's examine the logic of this method that had such an amazing success. The Holy Spirit is God Himself. As Christians, the Holy Spirit dwells within us. That happens when we became Christ followers. So as Christians, God already dwells within us. As Christians, we have been blessed with a close relationship with God.

Yet, how often in a day do we ponder the fact that God Himself dwells within us? How often do we acknowledge that the power of the universe is within our very being? And, how often do we try to comprehend the works of the Holy Spirit?

A New Method of Witnessing

What if the next method of witnessing would be for churches around the world to teach their people to pray for a greater understanding and outpouring of the Holy Spirit who dwells within. What if churches taught people to be less in control of their lives and more open to the leading of the Holy Spirit.

Christians would then sense a greater desire to be obedient to God, which would draw them closer. In being drawn closer to God they would be drawn into a greater quantity of God's perfect love. Then, because God's love is so beautiful and enriching, it will begin to automatically overflow.

People Respond to Love

This is the new method of sharing the treasure (God's love), simply because there is more love in us to share. The new method is witnessing through love. Love comes through being more intimate with God. Being more intimate with God comes through a closer relationship with the Holy Spirit. And a closer relationship with the Holy Spirit comes through prayer.

It worked with Jesus' disciples, and it is a model we should look into today. Other methods of evangelism are methods often taught without any consideration of the power and love of the Holy Spirit (God's love) flowing through us. They are just methods and often become mechanical. God's love flowing through us is more than a method. It is a mighty power that this world is so hungry to discover.

Let me share this example with you. We had neighbors who were not Christ followers. They were good people, they just did not know the love and joy of walking with the Lord. Every opportunity I had, I would try to befriend them. One day, knowing I was a Pastor, the man asked what caused me to quit a high paying job to go into the ministry.

I answered in a few sentences, talking about how Jesus changed my life, but did

LOVE, A HIDDEN TREASURE

not press the issue of him knowing Christ. Later they moved out of state. We called and asked if we could visit them for a day. He commented that we must really care about them to travel 200 miles to visit. God's love was drawing them.

However, while I was there, I blew it. Just before we left, I felt obligated to give the "bridge illustration", my method of witnessing. At about four sentences into the bridge illustration, I totally lost them. I finished but I'm not sure they were even still on the porch listening. God's love attracted them, my method turned them off. In this case I should have been satisfied with planting the seed, watering it, and then allowing someone else to harvest it.

People respond to love. The closer we get to God, the more unconditional love we will experience. The more unconditional love we experience, the more it will overflow. People will see that love and respond to it. It is so exciting to be around people who truly love us.

Sharing God's love is not taught by a method, it is simply an overflow of God's love within us. That love flows through us as we enter into God's presence and experience it ourselves. Then it goes out and touches others. What a simple idea. This new idea will become more than just a method. It will become a method empowered by Love--- God's perfect love flowing through us. Loving others is a "must" if we desire to share God's love. Witnessing has just been made simple.

LOVE, A HIDDEN TREASURE

Chapter 10
Epilogue

I have established in this book that God is the only source of love on this earth. Yet it still hurts when we sense an insufficient amount of love coming from those around us. This is an important issue. How do we train ourselves to not be disappointed when earthly love seems inadequate?

Ruth Myers in her book ***31 Days of Praise*** says it best in the following prayer:

> ***"Yet, Lord, I also thank You that even the people I most admire have flaws - that only You are wonderful through and through, with no ugly edges, and that***

LOVE, A HIDDEN TREASURE

people, even at their best, cannot meet my deepest needs. . .that at times they misunderstand, they disappoint, they expect too much, or they can't be available when I need them. This makes me even more glad to have You as my best Friend, my wonderful Counselor, my ever-present help in trouble- - -. How wonderful that I belong to You, the pure, unpolluted Source from which all downstream loves flow. ---whose love is flawless---"

Ruth is simply praising God for friendships that have failed because they help her appreciate the perfect love God has for her. As stated in Romans, God is able to take every bad situation we are confronted with, turn it 180 degrees and turn it into something good. What a pleasure to serve this amazing God.

Helping you discover God's treasure.

EPILOGUE

On my business card I have the words, "Helping you discover God's treasures." It is my passion to help everyone understand how special and fulfilling it is to serve God. My first book about "Joy" and this book about "Love" and my next book about "Peace" are all written to help the reader understand the treasures God has in store for us as we walk on this earth. He is not a judgmental God just waiting for us to mess up and then zap us. It is so special to serve God, so gratifying; and He always desires for us to live a complete and fulfilling life.

Experiencing God's love is a journey.

Just one final note about this book. Experiencing God's love is a journey. I dare say, it is something we cannot totally come to grips with on this earth. It is a quality of life we have trouble understanding because of the sinful nature within that keeps dragging us down. But, as we approach God

LOVE, A HIDDEN TREASURE

and experience more of His love, the journey becomes more joyful

Thus, I feel it is worth giving up whatever it takes to experience even a piece of God's unconditional love. Then, as I experience a small piece, it makes me hungry for even more.

Are you hungry to be loved unconditionally? Are you hungry to be loved even when you are in a foul mood? Are you hungry to be loved when you don't deserve to be loved? If you answer yes to even one of these questions, then you must approach God, the only source of love known to man. God will always love you unconditionally, because "God is love".

Amen, hallelujah, praise God ----------.